# Reclaim Your Spiritual Health

## Bishop Timothy J. Clarke

This work is dedicated to the people of God at First Church of God in Columbus, Ohio. You have loved, accepted and affirmed me. You have made preaching, teaching, and leading you a joy! I love you!

# Table of Contents

# Introduction

Several years ago I had an opportunity to attend a Friday night session of a local Alcoholics Anonymous (AA) meeting with one of my members. Like many of you I had seen bumper stickers that said, "Friend of Bill W," but I had no idea who Bill W was or why he had so many friends. I had heard of AA and the twelve steps, but that was the extent of my knowledge. That Friday night my eyes were opened to some powerful things. I sat in that meeting and thought, "I know that some of these people don't consider themselves a Christian, but I see more fellowship, more honesty, more transparency, and more acceptance in this AA meeting than I see in a lot of churches, including mine."

Many of you know that Alcoholics Anonymous is the grandfather of the twelve-step programs. It began as a mission and a ministry to those struggling with alcoholism started by a recovering alcoholic named Bill W. The foundation of AA is what they call the Twelve Steps.

I hope you will not take offense with my referencing the Twelve Steps of Alcoholics Anonymous in a Christian book when there are sixty-six books of the Bible to choose from. There may be those who think that because you don't drink alcohol that you have no addictions, but that is not true. I want you to replace the word "alcohol" with whatever your issue is—credit cards, sex, gambling, gossip, food, television, pornography, bad attitudes, jealousy, and so forth—because most of us are addicted to something.

Throughout the remainder of this book, I want to look at the benefits of a biblical understanding of how to apply the Twelve Steps to your life, your marriage, your relationships, your career, and your walk with God so that you may be able to *Reclaim Your Spiritual Health.*

# Chapter One:
## Living the Twelve Steps

*Step one—We admit we are powerless over alcohol; that our lives have become unmanageable.*

King Solomon wrote three books—the Song of Songs, Proverbs, and Ecclesiastes—and most Bible commentators agree that these books form a complete picture of the three stages of his life.

The Song of Songs was written when Solomon was in his youth—young, virile, and powerful. In his opinion there was no such thing as too many women, too much money, or too much fun.

Proverbs was written when Solomon was middle aged and a little more seasoned. He had experienced enough of life that now he had something worthwhile to say. I am convinced that Proverbs is Solomon at his best.

Ecclesiastes is Solomon as an older man looking back on his life—the wine, women, and the chasing of the wind—who begins to wonder what the meaning of it all is:

*I thought in my heart, "Come now, I will test you with pleasure to find out what is good." But that also proved to be meaningless. "Laughter," I said, "is foolish. And what does pleasure accomplish?" I tried cheering myself with wine, and embracing folly—my mind still guiding me with wisdom. I wanted to see what was worthwhile for men to do under heaven during the few days of their lives. . .Yet when I surveyed all that my hands had done and what I had toiled to achieve, everything was meaningless, a chasing after the wind; nothing was gained under the sun.* (Ecclesiastes 2:1-4, 11)

When I read the above verses, I think of step one of the Twelve Steps: "We admit that we are powerless over alcohol and that our lives have become unmanageable." Some of you have never had a drink in your life, but you are still addicted. The first step to victory is to admit you have a problem and that you can't handle it on your own.

If honest, you would have to admit that you face some things that you are powerless over. You put on a good front and pretend that you have it all under control, but the fact is your life has become unmanageable. Jesus Christ did not go to the cross so you could fake it through life. He came so that you could have life more abundantly. It is not God's will for you to go limping through life, barely making it.

## HOW TO TELL IF YOUR LIFE IS UNMANAGEABLE

<u>You have more, but you enjoy it less</u>. I call this the success trap. You thought achieving success would make you happy, but all it has done is add to your stress level. You have climbed your way to the top; yet, you don't know who to trust. You are surrounded by a bunch of barracudas who are already putting dibs on your office. If you tell people you are afraid, they will take your fear and use it against you.

You don't know who to tell your good stuff to because the people who used to be happy for you aren't happy anymore. The more successful you become the less some people can celebrate you. It is amazing how they can be happy for you when you are at a certain level; when you go higher people become intimidated and jealous.

Here is the other thing. You don't know how to act anymore. You move up in life and want to show people that you haven't changed so you still hang out and do what you used to do. Then they say, "I would think that since he has gotten up there he would act better. Look like she would

5

dress better with all that money she is making."
Then you decide you are going to dress better, act
better, and be more sophisticated. Then they say,
"Oh, so now you're trippin'." There are some days
you just can't win! Success is wonderful, but it has
a price tag and one of the price tags is not knowing
how to act. If you hang around one group, they
want you to act one way. If you hang around
another group, they want you to act another way.

You have all the trappings of success, but
there is stress that goes with it and that makes
your life unmanageable.

<u>You work harder, but it means less</u>. If you read the
entire book of Ecclesiastes, you will discover that
one of Solomon's fears was what would happen to
all he had worked so hard to achieve. Who was
going to get it all when he died? Solomon said that
one thing that makes life vain is that man works all
of his life and a fool inherits what he leaves behind.

Your life becomes unmanageable when you
work for the wrong reasons. Your motive for working is equally as important as the work that you do.
Sometimes you have to ask yourself, "Why am I
working so hard? Am I working to impress people,
for recognition, or to look better than someone
else?"

One of the ways you can begin to get your
life back in control is to stop letting your work rule

you. Your job is not your life. Don't believe me? If you get sick tonight, they are not going to close the company down. If you become disabled, they will not stop doing business because you can't travel anymore. They will offer you early retirement and then fill your position with someone who is able to perform the job. Since the company realizes they are bigger than one person, you better realize that your life is more than your job. Some of you work to the point that you neglect your family, health, and time with God. All you think about is work. You are stressed and under pressure. You are not sleeping or eating properly. You are working harder, but you are enjoying it less.

<u>You are trying to do it on your own</u>. If you ever read the *Big Book of Alcoholics Anonymous,* one of the things it says is to stop playing God. That is good advice for some of you. You act like you can solve every problem by yourself and that everything depends on you. You act like you are the only one who can get anything done. If you are living your life on your own strength, ability, power, and ingenuity, then your life is unmanageable. You are not smart enough or strong enough to handle everything that life will bring your way. You have to admit that every now and then you need help.

I could write an entire book on tenacity, but the bottom line is there comes a time when you have to hang up the phone, turn off the computer, turn off the lights, close the door, and go home. You are not a super person. You are human and you have to learn how to turn some things over to God. The only hope you have is to admit that you are powerless.

Unmanaged lives can lead to addiction. It is not enough to dress nice, drive nice, and live nice. Behind the scenes you are wondering why you are so unhappy, so unfulfilled. Why is your life unmanageable? You have the trappings—the house, car, career—and you are still unhappy. You are drinking too much and are tempted to start smoking again. You are watching pornography or have adopted some other vice. When your life becomes unmanageable, you start looking for something that is going to bring you pleasure or joy. The only place you can turn is to Jesus Christ:

> *Come to me, all you who are weary and burdened, and I will give you rest. Take my yoke upon you and learn from me, for I am gentle and humble in heart, and you will find rest for your souls. For my yoke is easy and my burden is light.* (Matthew 11:28-29)

Admit there are some things over which you are powerless and your life has become unmanageable.

The only real power that can break the yoke and addiction of habits is the power of God. Twelve step programs are wonderful, but if you don't have God while you are walking the steps, you are not going to make it.

## MAINTAIN YOUR FREEDOM AND DELIVERANCE

God is the Habit Breaker. It doesn't matter how long you have had a habit or how deep the habit has become ingrained in you. If you come to Jesus, He is able to step into your addiction, loose you, and set you free. You know that whom the Son sets free is free indeed (John 8:36). You must also remember to contend for the faith (Jude 3) and to stand in the liberty in which Christ has set you free (Galatians 5:1). In other words you must maintain your freedom and deliverance.

This is where a lot of people mess up. They are set free and assume that is all they have to do. Once you are free you have to fight to stay free. Once the Lord sets you free the devil keeps on coming at you. If you stand your ground, hold on and fight the good fight of faith, you can maintain your freedom.

One of the ways that happens is with the Twelve Steps. It helps many to stand firm in their recovery. You cannot spend a lifetime of getting into something and think that a twenty minute emotional encounter is all that it is going to take to get you out. It will take more than that.

You have to realize that your struggles don't just affect you; they affect other people. It is never just about you and it doesn't end with just you. That is why you must take inventory of your life and admit that while trying to balance career and family, success and salvation, things sometimes get out of control. So how do you get control back?

<u>Focus on a few things rather than everything</u>. You can't do it all. Do you know people who run from one thing to another? Every time you meet them, they are doing something new. That is what Solomon did:

> *I wanted to see what was worthwhile for men to do under heaven during the few days of their lives. I undertook great projects; I built houses for myself and planted vineyards. I made gardens and parks and planted all kinds of fruit trees in them. I made reservoirs to water groves of flourishing trees. I bought male and female slaves and had other slaves who were born in my house. I also owned more herds and flocks than anyone in Jerusalem before me. I amassed silver and*

*gold for myself, and the treasure of kings and provinces. I acquired men and women singers, and a harem as well—the delights of the heart of man. I became greater by far than anyone in Jerusalem before me.* (Ecclesiastes 2:3-9)

Solomon discovered what you will discover: You will never be happy until you narrow your focus. You can't do it all. Sit down and get a clear vision of what it is you want to do with your life. Where do you want to be in two years? Five years? Ten years? What is your vision? Watch what you run after. There is an old proverb that says that any man who chases two rabbits at the same time will miss them both. Decide which rabbit you are going after.

<u>Focus on what you were meant to do</u>. Philippians 3:13 has the Apostle Paul referring to *". . . this one thing I do. . ."* Do you know how to separate successful people from mediocre people? Successful people have determined the "one thing" they do. Michael Jordan is Michael Jordan because he focused on basketball. Tiger Woods is Tiger Woods because he focuses on golf. I was born to pastor First Church of God in Columbus, Ohio. In fact all that I do of any consequence comes out of being the Senior Pastor of First Church. Any books I write, any speaking I do, any impact I have is because I

have focused my life on First Church of God. I am happy and excited because I am doing what I was created to do.

You are no different. Your life will never be what it should be until you can say like Paul, *"this one thing I do. . ."* You may be able to do several things, but you were meant to do one thing.

<u>Focus on eternity, not immediacy</u>. Most of what Solomon did was for instant gratification, immediate pleasure, and imminent happiness.

You have to stop living like today is the only day you are ever going to have. If you want to live in the long term, ask yourself:

- What am I creating? What kind of home? What kind of children? What kind of relationships with family, friends, and God? What kind of financial future?

- What am I giving? What am I giving to my family and others? What am I giving to God and the Kingdom?

- What am I leaving behind? From here on out it is all about legacy. Steven Covey in *Seven Habits of Highly Effective People* encourages us to begin with the end in mind. If you were to die tonight, what would the preacher say is your legacy? What would friends, family, and the saints say about you? What would God say about you?

Step one of the Twelve Steps says that, "We admit we are powerless and our lives have become unmanageable." For many of you that is where you are. Like Solomon you are looking for what can only be found in God. It is only when you turn your life over to Him that your life will make sense. A verse from the song, *Only What You Do for Christ Will Last* by Raymond Rasberry, says it best:

> You can build great cathedrals large and small.
> You can build skyscrapers grand and tall.
> You can conquer all the failures of your past.
> But only what you do for Christ will last.
> Only what you do for Him will be counted in the end.
> Only what you do for Christ will last.

# Chapter Two:
# God Can!

*Step two—We have come to believe that a Power greater than ourselves can restore us to sanity.*

There are some stories in the Bible that would not have been included if it had been left up to me.  The following is one of them:

> *Twelve months later, as the king was walking on the roof of the royal palace of Babylon, he said, "Is not this the great Babylon I have built as the royal residence, by my mighty power and for the glory of my majesty?" The words were still on his lips when a voice came from heaven, "This is what is decreed for you, King Nebuchadnezzar. Your royal authority has been taken from you. You will be driven away from people and will live with the wild animals; you will eat grass like cattle. Seven times will pass by for you until you acknowledge that the Most*

*High is sovereign over the kingdoms of men and gives them to anyone he wishes." Immediately what had been said about Nebuchadnezzar was fulfilled. He was driven away from people and ate grass like cattle. His body was drenched with the dew of heaven until his hair grew like the feathers of an eagle and his nails like the claws of a bird.* (Daniel 4:29-33)

I have several issues with this story. The first is that it makes the Bible seem like a fairy tale. A man becomes like an animal, eats grass, and grows feathers and claws. This is more like an Aesop's fable than the Word of God.

The second issue I have is that it makes God look like a mean ogre sitting in heaven waiting for someone to make the least little mistake. God does all of this to Nebuchadnezzar just for ego tripping. Maybe the real issue is that I think about the times I ego trip and hope that God doesn't do that to me.

The third issue I have is that it shows the swiftness and severity of the judgment of God. I would much rather talk about God's mercy, grace, and love. I don't like talking about the judgment of God because I know that all of us deserve His judgment. If it were not for God's mercy, we would all be in a world of trouble.

All of these are legitimate concerns, but if we only focus on the concerns we are going to miss the beauty, power, and message in this passage and experience in the life of Nebuchadnezzar: The power of God to give back what we have lost, squandered and forfeited. It is about the power of God to give us a chance to start all over again. I am glad I serve a God who has the power to give me back what I have thrown away. Aren't you glad that the God you serve is the God of another chance? He can take the broken pieces of your life, the mess and the junk, put it back together and let you start all over again.

It doesn't matter what you have done, how far you have fallen, or how many mistakes you have made. The God you serve is able to take your mess and make it a miracle. When everyone else gives up, the God you serve is able to take you back and tell you that He still believes in you. If you will trust Him, He will make something beautiful out of your life.

That is what the Nebuchadnezzar's story is all about. It is not just about him messing up. The real story is about God putting his life back together again. Some of us are like Humpty Dumpty. We sit on a wall, experience a great fall, and all the psychiatrists and counselors can't put us back together. God is able to put you back together and help you start all over again.

This is what step two is all about: "We came to believe that a Power greater than ourselves could restore us to sanity." I was intrigued when I read this step because the confession of it is powerful by itself. Recovering people will admit that even though they were functional and able to go about the activities of their lives in the midst of their addiction, their behavior had become insane. Part of the sickness of addiction is the ability to fake it and manipulate others.

Addicts have to admit that they are sick. But all of us have been there. It may not have been drugs or alcohol, but all of us have something that when we look back on it we can say, "That was crazy!"

People with addictions have to admit that their behavior is not normal, sane, or rational. There is something sick about what they are doing. They have to admit that they cannot help or heal themselves. Part of the healing and deliverance comes from admitting that you need help and acknowledging that there is Someone who can restore you back to sanity. All of us must come to a place where we admit we can't do this on our own.

There is Someone who can help you. You are battling with an addiction and wonder if the cycle will ever stop. I don't care what you have done, the Good News today is that there is Someone who can help you and heal you. His name is Jesus. He can deliver you from any addiction, heal you, and set you free. What you can't do, God can!

## THE RESTORATION PROCESS

In Daniel chapter four we find Nebuchadnezzar, a man of power, prestige, and position who lost his grip on reality. He slipped into insanity and that is how the story would have ended but for God. What God did in Nebuchadnezzar's life is the same thing He will do for us when we are restored back to sanity.

God judged Nebuchadnezzar. To "judge" means to pass sentence, to assess and/or to take inventory. God looked at King Nebuchadnezzar's life and said, "I don't like what I see, and I won't accept what I see."

You may feel that you are justified in your behavior, conduct, and actions—there are some people who feel they have a right to live like they are living—but if God says it is wrong, it is wrong. You don't have the right to justify your behavior. You must submit to the judgment of God and tell Him, "I agree with what you say, Lord, and I will modify my behavior to line up." God could not restore Nebuchadnezzar to sanity until He judged him and let him know his behavior was unacceptable. God is saying that to some of you.

19

<u>God judges you based on His knowledge, love, and plans for you</u>. Other people may be able to get away with something that you can't. God's specific plan for you determines what you are allowed to do. There is no need for you to talk about what everyone else is allowed to do. When God has a specific plan for your life, He puts certain parameters in your life. Instead of complaining about what you can't do, embrace the limitations. It may be that He has something for you so awesome and great that He doesn't want to allow people to have anything to use against you to impede your progress.

<u>God never judges you without a reason</u>. I know you like to say, "I don't know why I'm going through this or having it so rough," but the bottom line is you do know and you don't want to admit why or own up to it. Stuff doesn't just happen to you.

Every time you sow a seed, it doesn't come up overnight, but it will come up. Some of you have been sowing nasty, mean seeds for years of gossip, rebellion, confusion, discourse, and so forth and now it is starting to come back on you. You can't throw out meanness and get back niceness. You can't throw out gossip and then reap someone speaking nice about you. You can't go around telling people off and giving them a piece of your mind (like you have that much to spare) and then have people sing your praises. If you are as mean as a rattlesnake, the same thing you put out is going to come back on you. You aren't catching hell just because it's hell; you are catching it because somewhere you raised some hell. Now that the table is turned and the shoe is on the other foot you can't understand why it is happening to you. Just ask God to remind you of what you were doing this time last year, because you will reap what you sow.

God never judges you without cause. When God judged Nebuchadnezzar, He wasn't just doing it because He didn't have anything better to do that day. On the surface Nebuchadnezzar's problem seemed small, but his sin was major. Nebuchadnezzar was filled with pride and God hates pride. Pride dethrones God and elevates you to thinking you are more than what you are. There isn't anything worse than a stuck-up Christian.

God never judges you without warning. Nebuchadnezzar had a dream that was a warning from God. When Daniel interpreted the dream, Nebuchadnezzar chose not to heed the warning.

If you are under the judgment of God now, there is no need in getting mad at God because at some point—normally several points along the way—God warned you about going the wrong way, messing up, or making a mistake. Now you are probably thinking to yourself, "God never said anything to me," but He did. God always sends a messenger. God has sent a Word to you through preaching, in Sunday school, through a television program, or one of your friends to warn you about messing up. You didn't want to hear it and rejected the warnings God sent.

<u>God never judges you without giving you space to repent</u>. When Daniel interpreted the king's dream, he said that he wished the dream was for one of Nebuchadnezzar's enemies. Then he said, "King, please, whatever you do get right with God, change your ways and turn back to Him." God gave Nebuchadnezzar space to get it right.

God is giving some of you a period of time to repent right now. In your sin God still has shown mercy because He continues to bless you and cover you even when you mess up. Some of you did things you had no business doing, but God didn't expose you. He still anointed you, helped you, still made a way, and still gave you favor. You were walking in disobedience and thought you were getting over on God. You weren't getting over on God; that is the mercy of God who is giving you space to repent. He said, "I am not going to cut you down right now. I could do it and I should do it, but I am not going to do it because I love you and want to keep you in the family. I am going to give you space to get your life together."

You don't have a long time to do it. You may have one more Sunday, one more message, one more time before God decides He has given you enough mercy, warning, and time. Now it is time for judgment. God gave Nebuchadnezzar a chance to change his ways; when he didn't do it, in one day the judgment of God fell on him.

God humbled Nebuchadnezzar. One moment Nebuchadnezzar is king, and the next he is in the field eating grass. Talk about a bad day! In Nebuchadnezzar's case, God caused him to lose things, be cut off from people, and become a spectacle. God didn't do it to destroy him, but to get his attention.

Every now and then God will let some stuff happen to you that will humble you enough to get your attention.

God changed Nebuchadnezzar. When the experience was over, God had his attention and had changed his life.

God will get you back on your feet. Sometimes you will weeble and you will wobble, but you won't fall down. Your knees may buckle and bend, but God will hold you up. If you go through it, God will change you.

Timothy J. Clarke

## A HAPPY ENDING TO A HORRIBLE STORY

The story of Nebuchadnezzar is filled with horror and drama, but it is also filled with hope and promise. When you read what happened to Nebuchadnezzar it is scary; yet, God planned it for his good. Have you ever seen God take what could and should have been a mess and bring good out of it?

<u>God puts limits on what trouble will do to you</u>. I like the story of Nebuchadnezzar because of all of the things that didn't happen to him. What happened was bad enough—crawling around like an animal, growing feathers and nails like claws—but no one killed him or tried to put him out of his misery. No one took his throne while he was temporarily insane. He didn't commit suicide.

When you are going through a difficult period, you don't need to only focus on what does happen, but on what doesn't happen. When you are finished listing all the things that *did* happen, turn the page over and write another list of what *could* have happened. You didn't lose your mind. You didn't lose your job. You didn't get put out in the streets. You didn't lose your possessions. You may have had a little bit of a setback, but you are still driving, you are still eating, you still have clothes to wear, and a roof over your head. You have plenty of reasons to be grateful.

24

God puts a limit on what trouble can do to you. God says, "This far and no further." You are still here because God put a hedge around you and only let so much happen. As bad as it has been, it could have been worse.

<u>God prepares a future beyond the painful present</u>. At the end of a seven-year period when God's calendar had been fulfilled, Nebuchadnezzar came to himself. He looked up to heaven and called on the name of God:

> *At the end of that time, I, Nebuchadnez-zar, raised my eyes toward heaven, and my sanity was restored. Then I praised the Most High; I honored and glorified him who lives forever. His dominion is an eternal dominion; his kingdom endures from generation to generation. All of the peoples of the earth are regarded as nothing. He does as he pleases with the powers of heaven and the peoples of the earth. No one can hold back his hand or say to him, "What have you done?" At the same time that my sanity was restored, my honor and splendor were returned to me for the glory of my kingdom. My advisers and nobles sought me out, and I was restored to my throne and became*

25

*even greater than before. Now I, Nebu-*
*chadnezzar, praise and exalt and glorify*
*the King of heaven, because everything*
*he does is right and all his ways are just.*
*And those who walk in pride he is able to*
*humble.* (Daniel 4:34-37)

That is good news for you. At the end of the ap-
pointed days, Nebuchadnezzar looked up to heaven
and called on God. His mind returned, his kingdom
was restored, and his counselors all sought him
again. They didn't see him as an animal; God gave
him dignity and honor and power.

God will do the same for you. This is the end
of your tests, trials, and tears. This is the end of
your heartache and disappointment. God will
return your mind to sanity, restore what the devil
took, and re-establish you.

The Lord has prepared something for you after your painful place. The days of poverty, want,
lack, and struggle have come to an end. People are
never going to see you the same way again. They
are not going to see you as a failure, as an unwed
mother, or high school dropout. God is going to re-
establish you, and let people see you for what you
are—a vessel of God, a vessel of honor.

# Chapter Three:
# Let Go and Let God

*Step three—We have made a decision to turn our will and our lives over to the care of God as we understand Him.*

Someone has observed that nothing is as painful as unrequited love. To love someone and not have the love returned is painful beyond words. Unrequited love affects both our emotions and our psyches. Most of us have had experiences of having a crush on someone, or secretly admiring someone, and not having those emotions returned. While it was painful and it hurt at the time, we soon got over it and proceeded to fall in love several more times.

When I speak of unrequited love, I am talking about when the love is real, mature, and directed toward your mate and it is not returned. Can you imagine being in a loveless marriage or a marriage where all the love flows only from one direction? That is the story of Jacob and Leah.

Jacob was a fugitive running from his brother, Esau, from whom he had stolen both the birthright and blessing. While in Padan Aram he moved in with a distant relative by the name of Laban who had two daughters, Rachel and Leah, with Leah being the oldest. The Bible says that Jacob loved Rachel, which isn't hard to understand. She was pretty, charming, sophisticated, and had the right shape and figure. She possessed everything that Jacob was looking for in a wife and he agreed to work for seven years to marry her. The Bible says those seven years seemed like just a few days to him. Then the story gets messy. The morning after his wedding Jacob discovered that Laban had sent Leah to his bedchamber in Rachel's place. When he asked Laban about it, he explained that the oldest daughter was to marry first. Jacob then agreed to work seven more years for Rachel:

> *When the LORD saw that Leah was un-loved, he enabled her to have children, but Rachel could not conceive.* (Genesis 29:31(a))

The word "unloved" is from the Hebrew root word *sane,* which means to hate personally, to be odious, express ill will and/or an aversion between a husband and wife. It is the lack of desire for contact or relationship with another person. That is what Jacob felt toward Leah. The sight of her made him sick, but God opened her womb and Leah began to conceive. She had baby after baby in an attempt to make her husband love her, but it didn't work.

In spite of the hatred Jacob had for Leah, he obviously got over it long enough to get her pregnant four times. He hated her, had an aversion to her, had no love for her, but at least four times Jacob got over his problem and had sex with her and she conceived. Just because someone will have sex with you doesn't mean they love you. Anyone who is willing to have sex with you, but who will not respect and affirm you is no good for you. That is part of the sickness in some of our relationships; they are one sided and that is not a relationship.

We don't go into relationships seeking what is in it for us, but a relationship that is worth anything should be mutually beneficial and fulfilling. Both parties should get something out of it. If all of your effort, energy, and time are going into making the other person happy and you are miserable, there is something wrong with that relationship:

> *When the Lord saw that Leah was not loved, he opened her womb, but Rachel was barren. Leah became pregnant and gave birth to a son. She named him Reuben, for she said, "It is because the Lord has seen my misery. Surely my husband will love me now." She conceived again,*

*and when she gave birth to a son she said, "Because the Lord heard that I am not loved, he gave me this one too." So she named him Simeon. Again she conceived, and when she gave birth to a son she said, "Now at last my husband will become attached to me, because I have borne him three sons." So he was named Levi. She conceived again, and when she gave birth to a son she said, "This time I will praise the Lord." So she named him Judah. Then she stopped having children.* (Genesis 29:31-35)

Leah did everything she could to earn Jacob's love, but there comes a time when you have to let go. There is also a time where you have to let God. After four children and no change in Jacob's affection, Leah finally had enough. She finally decided that the madness had gone on long enough. She was tired and she finally let go and decided that from then on she would praise the Lord. When you praise, you release God to work and do what only He can. Leah should have learned that after the second baby, but she didn't. She needed to let go and let God. When we begin to praise God, we release something in heaven and God begins to work. And when that happens, no one and nothing can hold Him back.

## **KNOW YOUR LIMITATIONS**

Leah had to learn painful and valuable lessons and make some important decisions. These are the same lessons and decisions you have to make if you are going to let go and let God.

<u>You can't change people</u>. Some of you knowingly married a knucklehead; someone with more issues than a newsstand, but you married them thinking you could change them. What you don't understand is that you don't have the power to change anyone. If people don't want to change, you can't make them. You are about to lose your mind because you hooked up with someone who was a mess when you met them and have been a mess ever since. You don't understand why they haven't gotten any better in spite of all your efforts. You can't make people better. If they don't want to be better, you can stand on your head, spit out silver dollars, and they will still do what they want to, because you can't change anyone.

<u>You can't control other people's response to you</u>. In other words you can't make someone love you. "Why don't you love me?" "What can I do to make you love me?" "If I change, will you love me?" "If I lose weight, will you love me?" "If I get a weave, will you love me?" "If I change the color of my eyes, will

31

you love me?" Here is the bottom line: If you have to change for them to love you, you will always wonder whether they love you or the modifications you have made in your life.

Leah had to understand that having a lot of babies would not make Jacob love her. No more than you doing stuff you know you should not do. Lowering your principles or dropping your standards is not going to make someone love and marry you. If they don't respect your convictions as a child of God, they don't deserve you. Because you are saved, you have to help people understand that you are worth the wait, effort, and energy.

Some of you are worrying now because someone doesn't like you. Get over it. There are several billion people on this planet. Everyone is not going to like you. Everyone is not going to be your friend or think highly of you. You have to make up your mind that their not liking you is their misfortune.

<u>You can only change yourself</u>. You can't change people or their response to you, but by the help of God you can change yourself. I want to challenge you to work on yourself. Be the best you that you can be and make improving yourself a top priority.

Step three of the Twelve Steps speaks to this principle in a powerful way: "We made a decision to turn our lives and our will over to the care of God as we understood Him."

## **LET GO!**

Sometimes you have to learn to let go. You can't fix things, change things, or make things right. It is time to let it go.

<u>Let go of the past</u>. Too many of you live life looking through the rearview mirror rather than the windshield. You make a wreck of your life and cause others to wreck as well. It would be bad enough if you just wrecked your life, but you involve other innocent parties in your wreckage. There have been times when because you could not let go of your past, you messed up your life and someone else's. They got killed from the fallout just from being around you. So what can you do to change things?

- Forgive. Until you are willing to forgive you won't move on. Whenever you are not willing to forgive, you become a hostage, too, but you have to forgive. It is going to hurt and it will be difficult. You will have to work through it and pray through it. But whenever you think you don't have the capacity to forgive, just look to the cross. Jesus forgave you, and He will give you the power to forgive someone else.

- Forget. I know every time you see them it brings back negative memories, but you will be miserable if you don't get past it. If you have children with your ex-spouse, you will probably interact for the rest of the child's life. Are you willing to get sick on the stomach every time you see your ex or are you willing to say, "God, I need you to cleanse my mind. Wash my memory." You don't forget in the sense that you get amnesia, but you forget in the sense that you give it to God so the pain is not recurring every time you see that person. You still remember what happened, but what happened doesn't control you.

- Focus on the future. You have to intentionally say, "That was then and this is now." Refuse to forfeit your future by focusing on yesterday. The future is too bright for you to throw it away because you won't let go of the past.

Let go of the pain. I have a friend, Howard Scott, Jr., who was involved in an accident at work where he lost part of one of his fingers. I was back in New

York shortly after the accident and I asked Howard how he was doing. He held up his hand and said, "Tim, it's the strangest thing. Sometimes, especially when it gets cold, it hurts where my finger was. It's not there anymore, but I still feel pain." Can you imagine trying to rub what is not there? If I hurt my finger, I can put my hand on the spot. But what do you do when the place that hurts is empty? What do you grab? What do you touch? How do you soothe what is not there?

Those of you who have been hurt by love know that the pain is real. It is like Howard's finger; it hurts, but there is nothing there. There comes a point where you just have to let go of the pain. There is healing for your pain, but there are things you have to do. Healing involves three stages: diagnosis, treatment, and time.

When you go to the doctor, the doctor or their nurse start with a series of questions: How long have you felt discomfort? When do you feel like that? Can you describe your symptoms? The questions are asked because they are trying to diagnose your case. If you want to get healed, ask yourself some probing questions: Why do I keep ending up in relationships like this? Why do I attract abusive people? Why do I keep drawing a certain type of person to me? Why are all the people who come in my life takers instead of givers? Why don't any of

my friendships last? You ask yourself probing questions to make an intelligent diagnosis.

After the diagnosis comes treatment. There is no need to take medicine for whooping cough if you have a broken arm. A proper diagnosis allows for treatment specific to your ailment, which then allows for healing.

You don't get healed overnight; it takes time. The doctor will give you medicine and instructions: Take three tablets two times a day for seven days. That doesn't mean that if you take the first three tablets in the morning you are instantly healed. When you take the second dose, you still won't be healed. But if you take the whole prescription, over a period of time you will get better. If you stick with the Word, stay in prayer, and stay focused on God, He will heal your pain.

<u>Let go of the person</u>. Someone hurt you, failed you, disappointed you, or let you down. If you are going to be delivered, you have to let them go.

- Resist the temptation to hate or get even with the person. "You wrong me, I'll wrong you back." "I will be staying awake at night plotting how to get you back." "I don't get mad, I get even!" That kind of mindset creates a vicious cycle in your life. When you get that full of venom toward one person, you can't turn it off. If you get that much anger and hatred in you toward one person, every time you see or think about them you want to hurt them. When you get so angry that every waking thought is consumed with how to retaliate toward that person, do you think you have the capacity to turn it off and only direct it toward one person? When you see one person and are full of anger, that same spirit is still in you. That is why so many of you don't have people in your life you can love, because you have focused your energy on one person and it spills over into all your relationships. You have to let them go. Resist the temptation to get back. Resist the temptation to hate them, even if you feel justified. Hate is a spirit that once loosed runs amuck.

- Refuse to respond based on their behavior. "You do me dirty, I'll do you dirtier." "You tell a lie on me, I'll tell a bigger lie on you." "You don't speak to me, I'll show you how not to speak. You're a novice, I'm a pro." You cannot respond based on someone else's behavior. Because someone does you wrong, you do not have the freedom to respond in the same way. Someone has to be the adult. Someone has to be a Christian. It doesn't matter what people think. What matters is what God knows, and since He knows your intent He will bless you. Sometimes you have to give up, give in, and back down. And if people take advantage of you, so what. Roman's 12:19 reminds us that, *"Vengeance is mine, saith the Lord."* Stand still and let the Lord fight your battle. Refuse to respond based on someone else's behavior. Decide that you are going to grow up. You are going to be the one with a level head.

- Release them so that you can be released. As long as you are holding someone in a certain place, you are being held, too. They can't go anywhere, but neither can you. You have to decide that you are going to release them so that you can go where God wants you. If you turn them over to the Lord, He will take care of your enemies and fight your battles.

## BEEN THERE, DONE THAT!

No matter who you are and what you are going through, you can always find a contemporary or companion in the Word of God. For every test, trial, and struggle you go through, someone in the Bible has already experienced the same thing.

If you have ever loved and not had the love returned; if you have ever been rejected by the one you love, if your love has ever been unrequited, you have a sister in Leah. The Bible says that Leah was in a loveless marriage. It was not just that Jacob loved Rachel more than Leah; the Bible says he didn't love Leah at all. You may be in a relationship where all the loving is one sided; you can learn a valuable lesson from Leah if you will only heed the warning.

<u>Let God change your perception</u>. Perception is your view and a lot of you see things the wrong way.

- Allow God to change how you see life. You have to understand the purpose of God for your life. You are not here by accident; you are here for a reason and a purpose. Your life has a purpose, goal, and ultimate destination. Life is not just about how much you can get. Life is about living for the glory of God so He gets praise out of your life.

- Allow God to change your perception of Him. Some of you have a skewed perception of God. Some people are scared of Him. God does not want you scared of Him; however, He does want you to fear Him. God loves you more than anyone else in this world. The Bi-

39

ble says, *"Perfect love casts out all fear"* (1 John 4:18). Some of you are scared that if you mess up, God is going to get you.

- Allow God to change how you see yourself. Leah's problem is the same as many people: She didn't like herself. Some of you have allowed the media to dictate how you should look and that is wrong. In order for God to change you, He has to change your perception. You must learn to see yourself the way He does—beautifully, fearfully, and wonderfully made (Psalm 139:14).

Sometimes the key to healing is changing what you want, what you go after, and who you want to please.

- Let God change your desire. Leah had to change what she wanted. She wanted to be loved by Jacob more than she wanted to love herself. There comes a point in your life when you have to allow God to change what you want. Some of you want to get married and there is nothing wrong with that. It may be that God will change that desire to where you want to be whole before you marry. The desire to get married is good, normal, and natural, but God will change your desire from marriage to wholeness before marriage. If you are not whole alone, you won't be whole married.

• Let God change what you go after. Many of you are going after the wrong things in the wrong ways. One of the things that we have to understand is that wanting things is not bad, but one of the tricks of the enemy is that he takes normal, natural, and even godly desires and twists and perverts them. In the end we go after a good thing in the wrong way. We do that with our need for acceptance. We all want to be accepted and loved, which is both natural and normal since God made us for fellowship and relationships, but when we lower our morals to get attention, we have gone after a legitimate need in an illegitimate way.

• Let God change who you want to please. A large majority of you are people-pleasers. The only problem is that people are fickle and they change every day. You will become schizophrenic trying to please people, because what you did yesterday to please them is not what they want today. Get to a place where you want to please God more than anyone else. That is what Leah had to do.

41

> She stopped trying to please Jacob and learned how to please God.

There are three ways that we allow God to change our needs; not one of them is easy, but each of them is a tumbler in the lock on your being who God made you to be.

- Let God change who you need. Some of the people you think you need, you don't. You think you can't live without them, but you can.

- Let God change what you need. The devil makes you believe you just have to have certain things and people, but he is a liar. You don't need the approval, acceptance, or affirmation of everyone in your life. You have let the devil convince you that you have a lot of needs, but you don't.

- Let God change what you think you need to make it. Leah thought she had to have Jacob's love, approval, attention, and affirmation, but she learned God can change your needs. You don't have to have as many people or as much stuff as you think to make it. Matter of fact, all you need is God. If people are on your side, that's nice. But if people walk out of your life, you will still make it. You must not allow your need for people, or their approval and acceptance, to determine your future. You are special all by yourself.

# Chapter Four:
## To Tell the Truth

*Step four — We have made a searching and fearless moral inventory of ourselves.*

Years ago there was a television show called *To Tell the Truth* which had three people all claiming to be the same person. There was a panel whose job was to interview the three people to determine who was telling the truth. After each panelist asked their set of probing questions, the host of the show then told them to decide who they believed was the real person. They would write down their answer and after a commercial break the show would come back on. The host would then say, "Would the real John Doe please stand up." At that moment the time had come for truth.

This is what step four is all about: Telling ourselves the truth. Too many of us are deceiving ourselves, and until we learn how to tell the truth, we will never be what God wants us to be.

As the Senior Pastor of First Church I have a dual role as a preacher and a prophet. As a preacher, I am to stand before God's people and say, "No matter what you've gone through, there is a God who is able to make sense out of the madness in your life. If you just hold on until tomorrow, God's tomorrow is better than today. No matter how low the clouds are hanging or how dark it is in your life, there is a bright side somewhere. If you just hold onto God's unchanging hand, the Lord will make a way somehow."

As a prophet, it is my job to confront God's people with the truth about their situation; to tell them when they are wrong, have sinned, or messed up. One of the challenges with the pulpit is that we are hesitant to tell people the truth because we are afraid they will stop giving, showing up, or liking us. A preacher cannot be so absorbed with being popular that they cease to be prophetic. I would rather you keep your money and I keep my integrity.

## SOMETIMES THE TRUTH HURTS

Psalm 51 is one of the more familiar and popular passages of the Bible because it deals with David's confession and repentance after his sin with Bathsheba:

> *Have mercy on me, O God, according to your unfailing love; according to your great compassion blot out my transgres-*

*sions. Wash away all my iniquity and cleanse me from my sin. For I know my transgressions, and my sin is always before me.* (Psalm 51:1-3)

It is amazing to me the people God uses in the Bible. If I were God, I don't think I would use David. Here is a man who didn't just commit adultery; he committed murder to cover up the adultery. I am glad that God looks beyond our faults and you should be, too. While we may not have done what David did, all of us have done something that makes us ashamed. I am glad God doesn't expose us or let people see the skeletons in our closets, aren't you?

Psalm 51 is autobiographical because David is telling the truth on himself. He takes a moral inventory of himself and doesn't like what he sees. When you do the same thing, you will get the same results. In order to get to the truth, there are several things you must do:

<u>Take a good, hard look at yourself</u>. It is important to remember that David didn't come to this place of honesty by himself. David had been going through the motions as if everything was okay and he would have stayed that way if God hadn't sent Nathan. David didn't repent because he decided he had messed up. He repented because Nathan con-

fronted him with what he had done and made him take a long, hard look at himself.

We don't want to do that. We are very good at pointing out the splinter in someone else's eye while ignoring the log in our own eye. We are very good at seeing the sins of other people and miss the sins in our own lives. We are very good at coming to Church and sitting in judgment of those around us when many times we are as guilty as they are, if not worse. A lot of people would rather look at other people than deal with their own demons. Whenever we look at ourselves we have to repeat the words of an old Negro spiritual, "It's not my mother, not my father, but it's me, oh Lord, standing in the need of prayer."

We can cover up, hide, and make excuses, but personal inventory reveals the truth about us. Taking moral inventory involves three things:

- The Word. Start reading the Bible and God will speak to you from it. So often we look at the Bible as this mysterious leather-bound volume that only preachers can make sense of, but nothing could be further from the truth. The Bible is really a saga of an intense love affair and how a being—God—goes after the object of His love—you and I. God has given us His Word so that we will know His will and so that we can follow and walk in

His way. Pray and ask the Holy Spirit to open your mind, heart, and ears to the things of God. He will make the Word come alive in you!

- Prayer. There is a difference between praying and just saying prayers. Saying your prayers is basically you giving God orders. But when you pray, you sometimes sit in the presence of God and not say a word because you are letting Him talk to you. When you get quiet before God, He will speak to you and when He does, He is not going to talk to you about someone else; He will talk to you about you.

- A real friend. Every now and then God will give you a real friend who will tell you the truth whether you like it or not. We need someone in our life who will tell us the truth, but most of us don't want a friend like that. We want admirers and not someone like Nathan who will say, "I love you, but you've messed up." One of my members, Louise Patterson (who has since gone onto glory), called me one day and said, "I love you, Pastor and I'm with you right or wrong." I said, "Oh, LP, that's nice." She went on to say, "When you're right, I'm with you because you're right. When you're wrong I'm with you

49

to get you right. But right or wrong, I'm with you." Everyone needs someone who will tell them the truth.

David had to confess to what he saw:

> *Against you, you only, have I sinned and done what is evil in your sight, so that you are proved right when you speak and justified when you judge. Surely, I was sinful at birth, sinful from the time my mother conceived me. Surely you desire truth in the inner parts; you teach me wisdom in the inmost place.* (Psalm 51:4-6)

There comes a point when we have to plead guilty as charged. One of the reasons this fourth step is so important is because in this step we have to look at ourselves and admit we are the one who is wrong. Most people don't want to do that. We would much rather blame someone else for our problems.

- Rediscover absolutes. If there is any one word that describes the tenor and tone of the day, it would be "relativism." This is a word that means nothing is absolute, nothing is right or wrong, good or bad; it is all relative and since it is all relative, we are free to do as we want, wish, and please. Not so! There are things that are just plain right or wrong. We have to develop a moral compass in our lives and say, "This is right and this is wrong, and if I do this, it's wrong."

- Submit to God's laws. God has set some laws in the world and you don't break them, you break yourself against them.

- Commit to obey God. It is not always easy to obey God. Obeying God is sometimes painful, difficult, and hard, but if you commit to doing it, then when you are challenged you can stand on the decisions you have made.

<u>Seek forgiveness and restoration</u>. The best news of the Good News is that you can be forgiven, you can be restored, and you can come back home: *"Create in me a pure heart, O God, and renew a steadfast spirit within me"* (Psalm 51:10).

Here is what blows me away: The moment David was ready to come clean was the moment God was ready to clean him! Hallelujah! Whenever you make up your mind that you are going to stop blaming other people for your problems and own up to your responsibility, you will discover that God is ready, willing, able, and waiting to bring you to a place of forgiveness and restoration. This is the place where you can be all that God wants you to be.

## FOLLOW THE STAR

One of the things that epitomizes the day and time in which we live is that we seemingly have lost our way. Someone has put it this way: "Mathematically we are in error, musically we are out of tune, and physically we are sick." We have more and enjoy it less. We get more and don't know what to do with it. We have the key to the store, but nothing in the store makes us happy.

A friend of mine told me of a break-in at a store where nothing was stolen. The thieves only changed the price tags on all the items so that a toaster that might have cost $20 ended up being $900 and a television set that might have cost $1,500 was tagged at $50. Isn't that the way it sometimes seems in your life, that someone has switched the tags and nothing makes any sense? What you need is a North Star, a constant that says, "This is the way to go, this is the way to be and this is the way you ought to live." You need something by which to order your life because you can't do it on your own.

This is why the fourth step—"We made a searching and fearless moral inventory of ourselves"—is so important because it reminds you there is a North Star. The word "moral" says it all. A moral inventory concedes the fact that there is a higher law than your wants and desires, even a law that is higher than your issues.

If you are going to live the way God wants, you must judge your life by that higher law and submit to the law and will of God. In other words, the world wants you to believe that you can chart your own course, do your own thing, have your own way, and still be happy. If you live your life your way, you will never be happy. You will make a wreck out of your life. When you live your life based on the will of God, it makes all the difference.

Since you have met Jesus and turned your life over to Him, hasn't your life taken on a whole new meaning? I am not saying you don't have struggles, problems, and pain, but even when God says no, you still give Him praise because you have power to handle your problems. You don't need to smoke, drink, get high, or overeat to handle problems. Every time you think you are going under something on the inside keeps holding you up.

That is why it is important to have a moral law to govern your life. It is not the law of the government, the Church, or your own personal rules and regulations; it is the law of God. That is why Psalm 51 is so powerful because David comes face-to-face with himself, deals with his sin, and receives forgiveness from God so he can move on.

All of us struggle with something. We will never break its hold and grip on us until we do this fourth step. We will never rid ourselves of the demons until we learn to tell ourselves the truth.

I am always haunted by the question Jesus asked that Gaderene demonic in Mark 5: *"What is your name?"* I know that it is more probable than anything that Jesus was talking to the demons in the man, but even that is revealing. When Jesus asked, what is your name? the demons answered: *"My name is Legion,"* which says to me that whatever controls you is what determines who you are.

Whatever you let dominate you is ultimately what determines both your identity and destiny. Only God can deliver you from the demon that is trying to control you. Isn't that often your story? You are Legion because you are often more than one person. You are one way on Sunday and another way on Monday; one way at Church and another way at home; one way in public, but your family knows you in a totally different way. You want to be one way, but you keep acting another. Most people at some point have wondered, "Who am I?"

## HINDRANCES TO HONESTY

All of us are Legion, and like David in Psalm 51 and members of AA, we must make a searching moral inventory of ourselves. Why is that so hard to do?

<u>You don't know yourself</u>. *"Surely, I was sinful at birth, sinful from the time my mother conceived me"* (Psalm 51:5). That is not David passing the buck or transferring blame or guilt. He is being honest. Some people want to pretend they have been a goody two shoes and have been in Church all of their life, which is not true. No one has been in Church all of their life; they may have been around the Church all of their life, but until you get saved you are not in the Church. And no one is born saved.

David said he was born into sin. Then he said he became a sinner by practice. Some of you have had a lot of practice. You must come face-to-face with your humanity. You have your treasure in earthen vessels and you will fail and fall. But don't get too happy. When you are saved, sanctified, and filled with the Holy Ghost, you don't practice sin. The blood of Jesus Christ cleanses you and the Holy Ghost helps you live a victorious life. It is not about you not being able to help it; the Holy Ghost gives you power to live right. When you come face-to-face with your humanity, it is only then that you realize how much you need God. When you do what David did, and see how frail you are, it makes you realize how much you need God. You can't live this thing called salvation on your own.

<u>You don't think you will be accepted</u>. Whether you admit it or not the opinion of other people does matter. One of your fears is that if people see the real you they won't like you, so you end up constantly reinventing yourself trying to make yourself acceptable. There is a difference between self-improvement and self-re-creation. You should want to improve yourself, but when you think that to get someone's love you have to re-create yourself that is going too far. The only problem is that you have changed so much you don't know who you are and people don't know who you are. No matter what you do everyone is not going to like you. I want you to give yourself permission to not be liked by some people. When you give yourself permission, it frees you to be you. It also frees the people God has in the world who will love you to be able to find you because you are the real you.

<u>You are afraid God won't accept you</u>. Sometimes Christians feel they have to earn God's love and gain brownie points with Him. Neither is true and neither is possible. *"But God demonstrates his own love for us in this: while we were still sinners, Christ died for us"* (Romans 5:8). God can never love you more than the day He saved you from sin.

David reveals a powerful truth: God knows you, He is aware of your mess, and He is willing to forgive you because He loves you:

*You do not delight in sacrifice, or I would bring it; you do not take pleasure in burnt offerings. The sacrifices of God are a broken spirit; a broken and contrite heart, O God, you will not despise.* (Psalm 51:16-17)

If you come to God with a contrite heart and tell Him you are sorry, He will forgive you. Remember that David didn't come clean on his own; Nathan confronted him. What blew me away is that Nathan didn't go to David on his own any more than David got right on his own. God sent Nathan to David. Nathan didn't know what David had done. He wasn't there when Bathsheba and David went to bed or when David gave the order for Uriah to be killed. God didn't send Nathan to David to embarrass him or to expose him. He sent Nathan to tell David it was time to come clean and confess so that God could forgive him, cleanse him, and help him move on. God couldn't use a dirty vessel so he sent Nathan to David. God still had work for him to do.

God sent me to tell you that He knows what you did and He still loves you. He wants you to come clean because He has something for you to do. He still wants to use you and bless you.

# Chapter Five:
# Coming Clean

*Step five — We have admitted to God, to ourselves, and to another human being the exact nature of our wrongs.*

I believe that one of the most difficult things to do is admit we are wrong. Parents don't like to admit it to children. Employers don't like to admit it to employees. Leaders don't like to admit it to those who follow them. Whether we are comfortable with it or not there are times when we are wrong and we have to learn how to admit it. I find myself in just that situation having to admit that in regards to a principle I have taught my congregation I have been wrong. Because I am a mature and growing Christian I have learned how to admit when I am wrong and own up to what I am wrong about.

Step five says, "We have admitted to God, to ourselves, and to another human being the exact nature of our wrongs." Here is where I need to confess and admit my error. I had been taught (and consequently taught it to others) that when it came to confession all we had to do was tell God and that would be enough. As I studied step five, I discovered that is not what the Bible teaches. In fact, the Bible seems to suggest that part of confession is not only being honest with God and ourselves, but it is also being honest with other people, especially the people we have wronged.

Step five is one we are uncomfortable with and goes against what we have been taught, especially in the areas of confession, repentance, and forgiveness. Matthew 6:12 gives us the model for prayer and a petition for forgiveness, *"Forgive us our debts as we forgive our debtors."* That one line suggests that our Christian confession has three components:

- Our confession should be daily. Just as we ask for daily bread we should also ask for daily forgiveness.

- Our confession should be direct. We direct our request to God. We also acknowledge that we are in relationship with other people, thus, our sins have hurt someone else.

- Our confession must be disclosing. We acknowledge our need to forgive as well as our need to be forgiven.

I am convinced that the truth of this teaching has the power and potential to change, if not revolutionize, our relationships. Think about it. How many relationships could be healed if someone would say, "I was wrong and I'm sorry."

## IT'S NOT JUST ABOUT YOU!

David begins Psalm 51:4 apologizing to God: *"Against you..."* which brings to mind a question I have often pondered. He apologized to God, but what did he say to Bathsheba about what he did to her? And didn't David need to confess that he had done wrong by Uriah as well?

Maybe you are not forgiven until you apologize to God and to the brother or sister you have hurt. A lot of us have done stuff to people, lied on people, mistreated people, used and manipulated people right in the Church. My question is what type of Holy Ghost do you have that allows you to treat people like dirt and never say you are sorry?

There comes a point when we have to learn that it is not enough to just confess to God, we have to learn how to confess to the person we have hurt. Some of you may have a lot of fence-mending to do. In the end the Word of God is our ultimate authority.

<u>Admit to yourself what you have done</u>. Shakespeare was right when he said, "To thine own self be true, and it shall follow as night doth day thou canst not then be false to any man." In other words, if you are true to yourself, you will be true to everyone else.

One of the challenges many of you face is that you are always trying to impress others with your reputation rather than seeking to develop your character. The difference between reputation and character is that your reputation is what people think you are; your character is what you really are. There is often a wide disparity between character and reputation. A lot of people have a good reputation, but they are perpetuating because their character has not caught up with their reputation. Your reputation is what you are in public; your character is what you are in private. When you leave the four walls of the sanctuary and are by yourself, what is your life like behind closed doors when the lights are out and no one is watching you? It is not what you do in a crowd; it is what you do by yourself that tells your character. Character is internal; reputation is external.

Sometimes the person you have the most problems being honest with is you. Admitting your guilt and culpability releases you. You are then able to do what God wants you to do. You can never move on until you are honest with yourself. All the stuff that has held you back and in bondage loses its grip when you admit your faults to yourself.

<u>Admit to God what you have done</u>. It seems like this should be the first thing we do, but the reality is that, like the Prodigal Son in Luke 15, we can't return to the father until we come to ourselves. The boy first came to himself and then went home to his father. We can't go to God until we first come to ourselves and then admit to ourselves that we are wrong. Admitting to God is necessary because it acknowledges that God is right, in charge, you can't live for yourself alone, and you are accountable to Him.

Ultimately all of your sins are against God because this is His world, you are His creation, and He has set guidelines and parameters by which you are to live. When you go against that, you are not just breaking the laws of man; you are breaking the laws of God. Confessing to God the exact nature of your wrong restores you. Admitting things to yourself releases you, but admitting things to God restores you. When God restores you, He gives you back what you have lost.

<u>Admit to another individual what you have done</u>. You don't like to do this, but it is necessary. God has formed us as family and we must all learn how to relate to each other, submit to each other and

confess to each other. Here is the beauty and power of doing that, especially to those we have wronged: It restores you back to true unhindered fellowship. That is why the devil fights it so much and makes it difficult to do, because he knows the power of reconciliation. Once a broken fellowship has been restored, it is like a broken bone that once mended is usually stronger at the place it was broken. When you admit your fault to another person, the Holy Ghost will bind you together and make you one. You will be stronger in your broken place.

## STOP SABOTAGING YOURSELF

There are times when you are your own worst enemy and do yourself harm in the area of confession and coming clean. At this stage in the twelve-step program, you have to get a sponsor. The sponsor is the person you love to hate, because they make you tell the truth and they confront things you would rather not face. If you are going to be healed, the sponsor knows you have to come clean. On the other side of confession, you will be all right.

What you hide can prevent or postpone your healing. Psalm 51 is powerful because David finally comes clean and stops hiding. He brought into the open what he had done. He didn't confess to the whole nation. He confessed to God and Nathan. This is the key. We have to know who to confess to:

- Confess to someone who is spiritually mature and can handle your confession. In order for a person to qualify as a sponsor, they must have at least three years of sobriety themselves. You can't help anyone until you get a track record yourself.

- Confess to someone you can trust; someone who can keep and hold a confidence. There is a story told of three preachers sitting on a boat fishing who decided that since they didn't often get a chance to talk they would confess something to each other. The first preacher confessed that sometimes he didn't hold his temper as well as he should and occasionally a curse word slipped out. The second preacher confessed that he didn't handle his money as well as he should and had bill collectors calling and checks bouncing all over town. The third preacher hadn't said anything so the other two encouraged him to confess something. He said, "You're not going to like this, but I have a problem with gossip and I can't wait to get back to town so I can tell everyone what you said!"

The moral of this story is that you need to know who is hearing your confession.

- Confess to someone who loves you and will still respect you after you confess. I don't want anyone in my life that after I come clean with them they start looking at me funny.

Things you hold onto can prevent or postpone your healing. In their book *Encountering Shame and Guilt*, authors Daniel Green and Mel Lawrenz suggests that sometimes we allow our shame to put us in bondage and our guilt to hold us back. We have to stop holding onto our past and our pain long after its time to let both of them go.

- Forgive yourself. This is not always easy. You think about things and replay them in your mind. There comes a point where you have to learn how to forgive yourself.

- Forgive those who hurt you. Learn how to say, "You did me wrong, but I'm going to make it. I can't hold you without holding myself so I'm going to forgive you and leave you in the hands of the Lord."

- Focus on what comes next. Something else is coming. You can't get it holding onto what has been:

> *Then I will teach transgressors your ways, and sinners will turn back to you . . . O Lord, open my lips, and my mouth will declare your praise.*
> (Psalm 51:13, 15)

David said that as soon as God dealt with his pain and past he would help someone else. When you surrender your life to God, He will take everything negative that happened to you and turn it into a blessing, even your failures and sins. When God cleanse you, He tells you to take what you learned and use it to help someone else. Isn't that what He told Peter:

> *Simon, Simon, Satan has asked to sift each of you like wheat. But I have pleaded in prayer for you, Simon, that your faith should not fail. So when you have repented and turned to me again, strengthen your brothers.* (Luke 22:31-32, NLT)

When a brother or sister falls, don't step on them. Reach down and help them up. The same God that gave you another chance is the same God that will give them another chance.

What you won't let God have can prevent or postpone your healing. Sometimes God has to hurt you to heal you: *"Let me hear joy and gladness; let the bones you have crushed rejoice"* (Psalm 51:8). God had to cut you open to let all the hatred, unforgiveness, and bitterness out because it was killing you. You might still have the scar, but the scar is the proof that what was in you is out and God is healing you. You might have been wounded, but God is making you whole.

- If you are going to let God heal you, you have to show Him the hurt. Remember when Lazarus died and Jesus didn't show up for the funeral? Mary and Martha both had an attitude, *"If you had been here. . ."* Jesus told them to show Him where he was buried. When He got to the grave, Jesus instructed them to roll the stone away. Lazarus came forth because when Jesus speaks everything—dead or alive—has to answer and obey (John 11:1-45). Stop trying to hide stuff and show Jesus where you hurt. When you show God the hurt, He has the power to heal you everywhere you hurt.

- Learn how to surrender the hurt. After you
show God the hurt, surrender it. Give it to
Him and take your hands off it. You have
carried it long enough; it is time to surrender. Now, to be honest, we don't always want
to do this. As someone said to me, "They're
my issues and I like them!" Sometimes we
like holding onto things, but victory, even
our deliverance, is always in surrendering it
to God. That, of course, requires trust and
we know that God is trustworthy. He always
has our best interest at heart:

> *"For I know the plans I have for
> you," declares the Lord, "plans to
> prosper you and not to harm you;
> plans to give you hope and a fu-
> ture."* (Jeremiah 29:11)

We can trust God to always love us, always look out
for us, and to always be there with us.

- Praise God while it hurts because it may not
get better right away. You may have to walk
with a limp for a while. You may have to
handle some pain. The Holy Ghost is a good
doctor. He knows that after He does surgery
and the pain medicine wears off, you are still

Timothy J. Clarke

going to cry a little bit, hurt a little bit, and that is okay.

# Chapter Six:
# Lord, Change Me!

*Step six — We are ready to have God remove all of our character defects.*

At the heart of the Christian message is the belief that people can change. Salvation, redemption, conversion, and justification are all words that deal primarily with the power and possibility of us to change, and the willingness and ability of God to change us.

Christians can look back over their lives and see the changes God has made since the day of salvation. We realize we are not perfect or haven't made a mistake since salvation, yet we know beyond the shadow of a doubt that what we were is not what we are. We have been changed by the power of God, and no one can make us doubt that Jesus Christ has made a difference in our lives. While we know we are still on our way and getting better, we can look back over our shoulder and see where the Lord has brought us from.

In order to understand step six—"We are ready to have God remove all of our character defects"—we have to look at it in light of step five—"We admitted to ourselves, God, and another human being the exact nature of our wrongs." What step six suggests is that once we come clean and admit that we are wrong, we then have to be willing to change.

If we were honest, we would admit that saying "I'm sorry" is something we do almost regularly. In fact, we have learned how to do it so well that it is almost second nature because we know all the time why we are apologizing. When I speak of changing, I am not talking about behavior modification. I am not going to teach you how to count to fifty and manage your anger. I am not going to teach you how to recite a slogan and modify your behavior. What I am talking about is what the Bible calls conversion—a radical, altering, transforming change.

Alcoholics Anonymous understands that in order for healing to be complete a person has to be willing to change, and change doesn't come easy. I heard a speaker once say that people don't resist change itself; they resist being changed. People are all for change as long as the change doesn't affect them. We can never be all we were meant to be until we are willing to change and be changed.

## HOW TO KNOW IF YOU'RE READY
## FOR A CHANGE

<u>When you can admit you have a problem</u>. In Psalm 51:1-2 David is positioning himself for God to change him because he is willing to admit that he has a problem:

> *Have mercy on me, O God, according to your unfailing love; according to your great compassion blot out my transgressions. Wash away all my iniquity and cleanse me from my sin.*

David used the words transgression, iniquity and sin. One would think that all David had to do was admit that he messed up, but David used various words because each one meant something different. He didn't broadly paint his problem and say, "Well, you know I have issues." No, David said, "I have sinned, I have transgressed, and I have iniquity in my heart." In other words, he confessed to messing up. Not that he *had* messed up, but that he *was* messed up.

You are not ready for God to change you until you are willing to admit that you have a problem. In many cases you are the problem. A lot of you have been through stuff and want to say that the way you are or act is because of what someone else

73

has done. The bottom line is at some level you have to own your own behavior. You have to admit you have a problem with your temper, tongue, appetite, handling money, whatever it is. You are not going to change until you admit you have a problem.

<u>When you get tired of living the way you are</u>. There is a story told of a dog sitting on a nail howling and yelping. The neighbor asked the owner what was wrong with the dog and the owner said he was sitting on a nail. The neighbor pointed out that it was obvious that the dog was hurting and wondered why the owner didn't pick it up. The owner replied, "When he hurts badly enough, he'll get up himself."

There are a lot of people like that dog; all they want to do is complain and transfer responsibility. But, when they get sick and tired of being sick and tired, they will let God change them. Some people don't hurt enough or want change badly enough, but when they do they will get up on their own.

<u>When you can see a way out</u>. Many people feel trapped in the hopelessness of despair. They think there is no way out for them, that they are destined to live life the way they are now the balance of their days. They look at themselves and feel that life has passed them by and it is not going to get any better.

The devil is a liar! Your life is not going to end like this. This may be a page or chapter in the story, but there is a difference between a chapter and the end of the book. It is time for some of you to put a period at the end of the sentence, close that chapter, and start a new one.

What God has for you is better than what you have right now. Yes, you might have messed up. Yes, you might have failed. Yes, you might have done something stupid. But that was yesterday and you are not bound by it. The God you serve is the God of today and tomorrow.

David said he wished he knew what to give God to make it right. He wanted to give him something that would eradicate his sin, but what could he do? Everything in the world belongs to God. If He wanted an offering, he would give some money. If He wanted sacrifices, he would kill an animal, but God wasn't looking for that. Then, David discovered what God was looking for:

> *You do not delight in sacrifice, or I would bring it; you do not take pleasure in burnt offerings. The sacrifices of God are a broken spirit; a broken and contrite heart, O God, you will not despise.* (Psalm 51:16-17)

If you allow God to break you (and then break you down), after He is finished, He will make you. After He hurts you, He will heal you. After He wounds you, He will make you whole.

# Chapter Seven:
# This Is A Job For God!

*Step seven — We humbly ask God to remove our shortcomings.*

When I was a child, one of my favorite television shows came on every day at four o'clock in the afternoon: *The Adventures of Superman* starring George Reeves. When there was a crisis in Metropolis someone would always say, "This is a job for Superman" and Clark Kent—a mild-mannered reporter for a great metropolitan newspaper—would then change into the man of steel. Clark Kent's co-workers were Lois Lane, Jimmy Olsen, and Mr. White. Whenever there was a problem the only people who could get in touch with Superman were Lois Lane, Jimmy Olsen, or Mr. White.

When I examined step seven I thought, "This is a job for God!" Every now and then there are moments when I have some situations that I can't fix, handle, or change. I need God to help me. Life has a way of bringing you to a place where you are between a rock and a hard place, the devil and the deep blue sea, and you don't have the ability to pull it off by yourself. You need help that can only come from God. I am so glad that when I need God, no one else has to get God for me. I can go to God for myself. I can call on Him and He will show up.

We were created by God and when there is something wrong with us we need to go back to God. We can't fix ourselves and there is no reason for us to try.

## NOTHING BUT THE BLOOD

Step seven says, "We humbly ask God to remove our shortcomings." That is something that only God can do. When Nathan confronted David about Bathsheba, David then went to God and asked Him to remove the defects from his life. Only after he took this initial action did he find the forgiveness and restoration he was looking for and needed. The same is true for you. When you go to God, you find the answer and the antidote for your problems—the blood of Jesus. Whatever your problem is, if you get some blood in your life, the blood can handle it. The blood of Jesus is able to do what medicine, psychiatric care, and counseling can't. There is power in the blood.

The blood cleanses you. The blood removes the stain of the sins you have committed. In the legal system it is called expunging the record, which is what happens when a criminal's offense gets removed. It lifts the offense off the record and cleans it so there is no evidence the offense was ever there.

Do you fully understand that when you came to Christ and asked Him to forgive you, one of the things He did was to cleanse your sin? God expunged your record and lifted the stain. If the devil goes back looking for something, he can't find a trace that the sin was ever there. You are clean.

The blood covers you. Some people have religion and not salvation, which is why they don't understand the wonder of being saved. They joined the Church, but they didn't meet Jesus. He makes a difference in your life. When you have had an encounter with Jesus, He changes you so that nothing about you remains the same. When you are forgiven, the blood of Christ covers your sin. When God looks at you, He does not see what you have done in the past; He sees what you are now and what you will be in the future.

Even after a criminal is pardoned and the record is expunged, there are some people who will look at them and still see a criminal. Not so with God. When God looks at you through the blood of Jesus, He sees you as the righteousness of God in Christ Jesus. When the blood covers you, God does not allow people to peek up under the covers.

<u>The blood converts you</u>. "Convert" means to change or to radically alter from the original state. It is what happens to a caterpillar when it becomes a butterfly. A caterpillar goes through a metamorphosis and changes from an ugly, slimy caterpillar into a beautiful butterfly. The caterpillar doesn't become a butterfly until it has been in the cocoon and struggles to break free. If anyone cuts the cocoon open before the butterfly's wing strength is built up, it will never be able to fly.

Right now you are a caterpillar struggling in a cocoon wanting someone to cut you out. The Holy Ghost wants me to tell you that blessing, power, and victory is in the struggle. If you don't struggle, you will never build up your wing strength and be able to fly.

# Chapter Eight:
# Making Things Right

Step eight — We made a list of all persons we have harmed, and are willing to make amends to them all.

Step nine — We made direct amends to said persons wherever possible, except when to do so would injure them or others.

Steps eight and nine teach us how to keep and maintain relationships, although the words are easier to read than to do. If we are going to live the kind of lives God wills and wants for us, we have to learn how to make and keep right relationships.

This is especially true of those who claim Christ as our Lord and Savior and call ourselves Christians. The very heart of our message, and the very core of all that we teach and preach, is based on the doctrine and message of reconciliation. The Good News of the Gospel is that we can come home, God is not mad at us, and our sin is not being held against us. If we learn how to live in right relationship with God, we also have to learn how to live in right relationships with other people.

The saints fall in love with Jesus, but can't stand one another. Yet the Bible says, *". . . Anyone who does not love his brother, whom he has seen, cannot love God, whom he has not seen"* (John 4:20). How can you love God whom you have never seen and treat me like dirt? Many Christians want to talk about their walk with the Lord and then walk by people and not speak to them. It is amazing how people will speak in other tongues but won't speak to you. If that is your definition of a right relationship, there is something wrong with that. If Christ is really in your life, He doesn't just help you love Him, He helps you love other people.

This is why these steps are so important; they make us realize that we have a religion that is both vertical and horizontal. Our lives must be lived in proper relationship not only with God but with other people.

Steps eight and nine are very challenging, which may explain why so many people are willing to live in isolation, separation, and estrangement. The steps are difficult and costly, but they are necessary if you are going to be reconciled in your relationships.

- Admit what you have done. If you are going to make your relationships right, the first thing to do is admit that your actions, conduct, and behavior have caused the people you love (and who love you) pain.

- Admit that what you did was your fault. You are reaping the seeds of your own planting. You can't blame it on anyone else.

- Apologize and seek to make things right. There are some things that you can't leave undone. There are some issues that need closure. There are some relationships that must be repaired.

There are some people who believe that their past is the past and since God has forgiven them they don't have to go back and make things right. Yes, you are forgiven. Yes, your past is behind you. But you have to remember the following:

- You can't undo the past. The challenge with reconciliation is that you are trying to undo what has been done and you can't. Instead focus on trying to make amends for what was done.

- You can't make the pain go away. Even after you apologize people may still be hurt. You have to allow them that privilege if they are going to be healed. Just because you came to a place where you are ready to apologize does not mean they are instantly at a place where they are ready to accept it. It took you time to come to the place to apologize; give them time to allow God to heal them so they can get past it. They are not on your schedule.

- You can't make people forgive or accept you. If you hurt someone and apologize, you can't make them forgive you. You are not responsible for their reaction; you are only responsible for your action. If they reject you, don't think you failed or it was a waste of time. You did what you were supposed to do. Turn the situation over to God so that in His time He will deal with them. You may be in an estranged relationship where what you did hurt someone so deeply they may never fully forgive you. You are going to have to live with the tension of a strained relationship. It may be uncomfortable, but it is where you are. Things may never be the same. You did the right thing and you are not responsible for what they do. Having said that, it is still important that you seek to make amends and heal the broken relationships in your life.

## WHY MAKE AMENDS?

We need to make amends because relationships are important. In the Sermon on the Mount (Matthew 5, Luke 6), Jesus spent a lot of time talking about the value and importance of relationships. He talked about how to treat people, how to talk to them, and how to treasure them. Jesus said your relationships validate your worship because your worship is not acceptable to God if you don't treat people right. You were made and created for relationships. You need and desire relationships. What makes your life worthwhile is not money or things, but people. Relationships are important to God.

<u>Relationships are fragile</u>. All of us have seen packages marked, "Fragile: Handle with Care." I have often thought that we need to stamp that on people and relationships.

- Relationships involve fragile human beings. Just think how easily you can be hurt and offended. All it takes is for someone you love to say something wrong and it will mess you up. You may put up a good front, but your roughness and gruffness is really to hide just how tender you are.

- Relationships unfold in life experiences. Things happen, and change comes every day. You don't live in a vacuum; you live in the context of life experiences.

- Relationships are subject to the changes of life—sickness, setbacks, disappointments, and death. Relationships get messed up when you try to keep people in a time warp. You still want them to be the person they were when you first met them. It is not going to happen. You are not the same, and you don't need anyone to judge you today based on how you were yesterday.

Relationships are more important than anything else. Jesus said that reconciliation is more important than an offering:

> *Therefore, if you are offering your gift at the altar and there remember that your brother has something against you, leave your gift there in front of the altar. First go and be reconciled to your brother; then come and offer your gift.* (Matthew 5:23-24)

# Chapter Nine:
# Know Yourself

*Step ten — We continue to take personal inventory, and when we are wrong promptly admit it.*

Steps ten, eleven, and twelve are often called the maintenance steps. They exist to help those in recovery maintain their recovery.

Step ten is closely akin to the Christian life. Those in twelve-step programs are coming out of addiction into recovery and are on the same path as those of us who are walking with the Lord. The reason I say that is because those of us who are saved have come out of lifestyles that were wrong, harmful, and destructive. Now we are living a life we have never lived before. In other words, we are in a process and we need to learn how to thank God for the victories along the way.

People involved in twelve-step programs understand that their recovery is a process. That is what messes up the saints. The saints always talk about salvation as an event, although indeed it was a one-time event. Your salvation is separate from your walk with God, which is a life-long process. That is why people in recovery never talk about being an "ex" anything. They say they are "recovering," because they understand that if they don't stick to the plan, they can slip back into old habits.

Since people in recovery have a plan for staying clean, you need to have a plan for staying saved. The devil will throw stuff at you that, if you are not careful, will make you change your mind. If you don't have a plan, you are not going to make it. Anything you do in life you have to have a plan for, whether buying a house or car or even losing weight. The plan for staying saved is to go to Church, read your Bible, and pray. Jesus works salvation in, but we have to work it out.

## IT'S ALL A PROCESS

Step ten says, "We continue to take personal inventory, and when we are wrong promptly admit it." The key word in step ten is "continue." Once you start you have to stay with it and build on what God has done in your life. Continue to grow in your knowledge and relationship with God. It doesn't happen overnight.

Learn how to examine yourself. Self-examinations are painful but necessary. When conducted in the hands of a skilled professional, it may deter some things from happening. Really looking at yourself, probing and taking personal inventory is not painless, enjoyable, or easy. It is a necessary hurt. I am talking about looking at yourself in a long, hard way and concluding, "This is the truth about you." It hurts when you have to look at yourself and admit that you are the problem because it is easier to blame other people. A medical professional will use different instruments for your examination: the stethoscope, penlights, blood pressure cuffs et cetera, but what do you use? When you get ready to examine yourself, use the Word. When you read the Word, you don't argue with what you see, you just do what the Word says. The Word is not going to change.

Learn how to judge yourself. To "judge" means to evaluate, form an opinion, and make a ruling on an issue. In the court system, the judge makes a ruling either for or against you based on the evidence presented and the standard of the law already set. There are times when you need to sit in judgment of yourself. If you would judge yourself, you could avoid some hurt and pain that you bring on yourself and inflict on others. Sometimes it is as simple as judging your talk, language, attitude, conversation, and motives. It means saying to yourself, "You're wrong." The purpose of an exam is to show what is wrong, but it doesn't correct what is wrong.

Years ago I had a car that left a lot to be desired. The car had engine problems and caused me a lot of frustration. What I wanted to do was push it off a cliff, but then I wouldn't have transportation. So, instead, I washed it and cleaned it up real good. It looked nice when I finished, but I realized that the car still had engine problems, only it was cleaner. That is what you do sometimes. You deal with surface stuff when it is your heart that has the real problem. You try to clean it up, buy new clothes, or get a new hairstyle thinking that will solve the problem, but that is like washing a car with a bad engine. You haven't done anything except address the surface issues. When you examine yourself, you find out what the problem is and then you take steps to deal with the problem.

Learn how to submit yourself. When you won't examine or judge yourself, God will do it for you. If you submit to what God says about you and accept His judgment, you will avoid the condemnation coming into the world. Step ten sets us free from guilt and condemnation. If I examine myself every day, there is no way I can be mad at you for ten years. If I am constantly examining and judging myself, there is no way to be at odds with one another. If I have a problem with someone and the

Holy Ghost brings it to my attention, I have no choice but to go to that person to make things right. When that happens, we stop the devil's scheme to bring division in the Church.

# Chapter Ten:
## Knowing the Will of God

*Step eleven — We have sought through prayer and meditation to improve our conscious contact with God as we understand Him, praying only for knowledge of His will for us and the power to carry that out.*

As you mature, you discover that you don't need as much as you thought. Your drive, ambition, needs, and desires should undergo an amazing transformation. As a younger man, I thought that having a lot of clothes would make me successful and happy. I have lived long enough to discover that you can get all of the "stuff" and still be unsuccessful and unhappy.

The sign of a mature person is their ability to decide what is really important in life. I am not sure who wrote the following poem, but I have often quoted it:

When we are young, we want the whole world.
When we get older, we want a piece of the world.
As we get wiser, we want our corner of the world.
At the end of life, we'll settle for six feet of the world.
And that's just what you get.

Life brings changes. You can tell where a person is and what their life is about by what they want out of life. A good example of this is the Apostle Paul. In Philippians chapter three, Paul gives us his resume where we discover he walked away from power, prestige, and position to find what he really wanted and needed. That is what I mean by as you mature the things you want change. One of the most sobering lessons of life is that "things" will never truly satisfy you. Sometimes the more you have the less satisfied you are.

## "NEED" VERSUS "WANT"

The book *Integrating Spirituality into Treatment: Resources for Practitioners* edited by William R. Miller says, "In the third step we surrendered our lives to God because we had to. We had come to the end of ourselves and we had nowhere else to turn."

In other words, we came to God because we needed to; now we come to God because we want Him in our lives.

There is a difference between needing God and wanting God. You need God all the time because you can't do anything without Him. But there comes a point in your life where you don't serve God because you need Him; you serve Him because you want Him.

Have you ever been in a relationship where you sensed the only reason the person was still with you was because they needed you? You were the difference between living in a house and living on the streets. When you are in a relationship only because you are needed, it makes you feel like you are being used.

Do you know what it is like to be in relationships because you are wanted? The person is with you because they love you. You don't have to do anything for them because just being with you is enough. There is a difference between being with someone out of need versus want.

In step eleven you seek to improve and enhance your conscious contact with God. The God who saved you out of the hell of your addiction is no longer just the God you need; He is the God you want.

That is what Paul talks about in Philippians chapter three. He wanted an experience, encounter, and relationship with God. Isn't that what you want as well? Don't you want to know God in a real way? Isn't that why you go to Church, pray and read the Bible? You want to know God.

Deep down your desire, wish, and hope is to know God. Here is the good news: God wants you to know Him and He wants to know you intimately and personally. That is why you can have hope. There are three ways that can happen:

<u>Desire</u>. "Desire" is defined as longing, craving, wanting:

> *What is more, I consider everything a loss compared to the surpassing greatness of knowing Christ Jesus my Lord, for whose sake I have lost all things. I consider them rubbish, that I may gain Christ and be found in him, not having a righteousness of my own that comes from the law, but that which is through faith in Christ— the righteousness that comes from God and is by faith. I want to know Christ and the power of his resurrection and the fellowship of sharing in his sufferings, becoming like him in his death, and so, somehow, to attain to the resurrection from the dead. (Philippians 3:8-11)*

Paul was passionate about wanting to know God. You have to be passionate about your desire to know God, too. You can't know God just going to Church, sitting on a pew, going through the motions. You have to want Him. When you want Him, it will make you do things you never dreamed of doing. Some of you don't really want to experience God in spite of what you say, because you are not willing to do what it takes to experience God.

Do you know how you experience God? Through worship. Worship is one of the ways we access God. In fact, it brings us into His presence in a wonderful and powerful way. Worship lifts our thoughts and our hearts toward God and we encounter Him in a transforming experience that changes us.

It is what happened to Isaiah when he saw the Lord high and lifted up (Isaiah 6:1). That vision awed him, humbled him and changed him. A true encounter with God will do the same thing to and for us.

Discipline. You will wait and work for what you really want. In fact, you will sacrifice for what you really want. Paul realized that in order to gain what he wanted he had to give up what he had. Our friends in the twelve-step programs know this well. You can't be drunk and sober. You can't use drugs and be clean. You can't gamble and abstain. You have to give up one to have the other. You can't be a recovering person and still do the things you are supposed to be recovering from!

In order to know God, Paul had to give up a religion that no longer had power. Paul understood it took discipline. God will help you, but sometimes you have to help Him. Here is how you do it: You stay away from stuff that tempts you. If drinking is your problem, don't move next door to the liquor store. If you are a crack addict, stay out of the crack house. It is good to know that God will be there if you fall, but it is even better to know that you don't have to fall at all. God is able to pick you up when you fall and He is also able to keep you from falling.

Determination. It is all about perseverance. You must have a made up mind and a determination to just go on:

> Brothers, I do not consider myself yet to have taken hold of it. But one thing I do; Forgetting what is behind and straining toward what is ahead, I press on toward the goal to win the prize for which God has called me heavenward in Christ Jesus. (Philippians 3:13-14)

The image that Paul uses is of a runner straining to cross the finish line. There is only a short distance to go and it all comes down to this part of the race. A runner stretches (presses) because he has to make it. You have to make it, too. Be determined that no matter what it takes or what it costs, you are going to make it.

# Chapter Eleven:
## A Story to Tell

*Step twelve — Having had a spiritual awakening as the result of these steps, we have tried to carry this message to alcoholics and to practice these principles in all our affairs.*

One reason we have examined Psalm 51 so often in this book is because David really was a man in recovery. He was seeking health, healing, wholeness, and sanity, just like we are. David wanted to tell others what God had done for him.

This is what the twelfth step is all about. Having now been touched and transformed by God you are ready to tell someone else. Pay close attention to the opening—having had a spiritual awakening—because it is important to understand that any recovery from addiction must have about it a spiritual component.

If you are going to be set free, you have to do more than wish yourself free; it is going to take the power of God to set you free. There will be no permanent improvement in your life without the anointing, assistance, and aid of the Holy Ghost. Just think how many times you have tried on your own to break a habit and you will realize I am right. When you finally gave your addiction to Jesus and laid it at the foot of the cross, you can testify that He broke the chain and power of the addiction and now you are free. I don't care what your bondage is, there is a Bondage Breaker named Jesus Christ who can set you free.

The people in AA know that after having a spiritual awakening—not an emotional, intellectual, or physical awakening—they now are ready to share with others what God has done for them. They had an encounter with God and it transformed their lives. All of us, no matter who we are, where we come from or what the particulars are of our situation, have a story to tell and a testimony to give about the goodness of God in our lives.

## LEARN TO BECOME A STORYTELLER

This twelfth step encourages you to share your testimony, not just for the sake of those you share with, but for your own sake as well. When you share your story, it doesn't just bless the people who hear it, it will bless you when you tell it.

- Telling your story keeps fresh in your mind what God has done for you. There is nothing worse than a saint with amnesia. The devil doesn't want you to tell your story because it keeps fresh in your mind just how far God has brought you.

- Telling your story makes you grateful for what you have experienced. When you have a bad day, it is easy to slip into self pity. When that happens, one of the best ways to bring yourself out of it is to start telling someone what the Lord has done for you. When you start thinking about what God has done for you, it will make you grateful in spite of your present condition. You may not have all that you want right now, but things sure are better than they used to be.

- Telling your story reminds you of where you came from. Most of the saints I know like to revise or modify their life story. If you listened to some of them talk, you would think they were only twenty years old because all they talk about is the last twenty years of their life. The only problem with that is they are giving an abbreviated biography. What makes others excited is knowing where you came from. The real celebration is not what you have now. You can only appreciate what you have now when you compare it to what you had in the beginning. You need to tell your story as much as it needs to be told, because it keeps your heart warm and your spirit grateful.

## A STORY WORTH TELLING

While all of us have a different story—based on experiences that are unique to us—there are none-theless common threads that weave their way through each of our stories. We have all sinned, strayed, and sought to find our way back home. We might not be able to tell each other's story, but we can recognize and identify with each other because we can relate to each other's journey. That is why when someone testifies about being saved out of addiction, someone who has never known their particular addiction can still rejoice with them because they have been saved, too. You don't need to have the same story to rejoice; you just need to remember what you were saved from. What makes the Church so powerful is that everyone has a story.

A story of redemption. "Redemption" is one of the most beautiful words in the Christian language. It means to buy back. It means to pay a ransom. It means you were kidnapped and held against your will; the devil sent God a ransom note and demanded a payment. God said He loved you enough to pay the price and sent His Son Jesus Christ.

When God wanted to show His love for Israel, He used a prophet by the name of Hosea and had him marry a prostitute. Can you imagine belonging to a Church where the First Lady is a hooker? That was Hosea. When Gomer went back to harlotry and Hosea wanted to divorce her, God had Hosea buy Gomer back. He had to redeem her from the public auction block where everyone would know what Gomer had done. When Hosea didn't want to do it, God reminded him that it wasn't about him: "I'm trying to paint a picture of how much I love my people because they're a lot like your wife. They've gone whoring after other gods and committed harlotry with other gods, but I still love them."

Isn't your story a story of redemption? You may not have prostituted your body, but you prostituted your convictions, standards, morals, teaching, and upbringing. In your mess God still loved and redeemed you. God came in Christ to where you were, and in your sin He paid the ransom and redeemed you.

A story of rescue. The reason I use the word "rescue" is because you were unable to save yourself. You couldn't pull yourself out of what you were in;

you needed Someone to save you. You needed Someone to rescue you.

When David sinned, God sent Nathan because David couldn't get himself out of the predicament he was in; he needed help and so do you. You can't save yourself. Even the desire to be saved doesn't come from you. If you're saved today, it is because God came looking for you. You didn't have enough sense to go looking for Him. God took the initiative and came to the mess you were in and saved you. That is why Jesus told the story in Luke 15 of the shepherd who would leave ninety-nine sheep to go looking for the one that was lost.

When I was a much younger preacher, my wife would often sing *Somebody Saved* Me by H. J. Ford as the sermonic hymn:

> Someone saw me when I was drifting.
> Out on the desert loaded with sin.
> Someone saw me and with compassion.
> Spoke to me gently bade me come in.
> Someone saw me.
> Oh, it was Jesus mighty to save.

Brothers and sisters that is your story. When you were drifting and sinking, straying and wandering, Someone came looking for you and it was Jesus.

A story of restoration. Thank God He redeems and rescues you. He also gives back what you lost by accident, what you squandered by ignorance, and what you gave away. There are some things you gave away to the devil, the world, your addiction, and your previous lifestyle. You never thought you would see them again. The wonderful thing about the story He gives you is that when you come back to God, He restores the things you thought you would never have again. When Jesus comes into your life He gives you back joy, hope, dreams, opportunities, and position. He restores you back to Himself and your loved ones. He restores back to you everything you thought you had lost forever.

Let me tell you how I know. There is a marvelous story in the Bible about the Gaderene demoniac who lived in the cemetery among dead people. People tried to bind him with chains and he plucked them apart. They tried to bind him with fetters and he broke them like tissue paper. One day Jesus looked at him and asked, *"What is your name?"* Before he could answer the demons answered *"Legion. There are many of us in here."* Jesus was not threatened by the presence of the demonic and told the man, "I'm going to make you whole," and drove the demons out of the man. The man wanted to follow Jesus, but He told him to go back among his own people. Jesus wanted to use him as an ambassador to show people how He could take the vilest person and clean them up. The man went back home and every time he walked around the neighborhood, people saw him and whispered among themselves, "Isn't that the man who used to live in the cemetery?" (Mark 5:2-20)

When Jesus comes in your life He doesn't just deal with you in a one-dimensional way because you are tri-pod person—body, mind, and spirit. The Bible says the man was clothed; that is his physical. He was in his right mind; that is his mental. He was sitting at the feet of Jesus; that is the spiritual.

Step twelve says, "Having had a spiritual awakening as the result of these steps, we tried to carry this message to alcoholics and to practice these principles in all our affairs." That is how it ends. It starts with God because your life was out of control, and it ends with God because He has given you a story.

- A story of redemption: He paid the ransom.
- A story of rescue: You couldn't save yourself.
- A story of restoration: He has lovingly given back to you what you thought you would never get back.

God has graciously allowed you to *Reclaim Your Spiritual Health.*

# Appendix

THE TWELVE STEPS OF ALCOHOLICS ANONYMOUS

1.   We admitted we were powerless over alcohol, and that our lives had become unmanageable.

2.   We came to believe that a Power greater than ourselves could restore us to sanity.

3.   We made a decision to turn our will and our lives over to the care of God as we understood him.

4.   We made a searching and fearless moral inventory of ourselves.

5.   We admitted to God, to ourselves, and to another human being the exact nature of our wrongs.

6.   We were entirely ready to have God remove all these defects of character.

7.   We humbly asked Him to remove our shortcomings.

8.   We made a list of all persons we had harmed, and became willing to make amends to them all.

9.   We made direct amends to such people wherever possible, except when to do so would injure them or others.

10.  We continued to take personal inventory and when we were wrong promptly admitted it.

11. We sought through prayer and meditation to improve our conscious contact with God as we understood Him, praying only for knowledge of His will for us and the power to carry that out.

12. Having had a spiritual awakening as the result of these steps, we tried to carry this message to alcoholics, and to practice these principles in all our affairs.

Please enjoy this excerpt from *Caution! God at Work: Trusting God through Tough Times*
ISBN 978-0-9764022-5-1.

From time to time every preacher finds themselves asking the age-old question of what shall I preach? The genesis of that question is not found in the scarcity of preaching material, but rather a desire on the part of the preacher to meet a real need in the life of the worshiper. The preacher's goal is for those who sit under their preaching to be confronted and comforted by the claims and promises of God.

I suppose in some ways those of us who preach the Gospel can find comfort in knowing that we are not the first to raise this question. In fact, the question is as old as the prophet Isaiah: *"A voice says, 'cry out.' And I said, 'What shall I cry?'"* (Isaiah 40:6), which only goes to show that even the prophet occasionally found himself stymied as to what he should preach. I have to confess that after preaching for over thirty-five years that every now and then I find myself wondering, "What can I say that I haven't already said?" and the answer came to me as I was rummaging through the Word of God.

All of us have seen those signs that read, "Caution: People at Work," which serve as a reminder for us to slow down, be more alert and aware because there are men and women on the road working. You may be upset that you have to slow down because they are working, but what you have to remember is that they are working for your good. I hate seeing the orange barrels because they usually mean that it is going to take longer for me to reach my destination. I have to slow down for a temporary inconvenience while people are working on a permanent improvement. Sometimes the road work is hidden behind a canopy and you can't see what is going on. You must understand that while God may have you slowing down, and while you may not be making the progress that you want to make, you can still celebrate the fact that God is at work. And if God is working, He is always working for your good, even when you cannot see it.

*Caution! God at Work* is meant to bring hope to Christians who find themselves in difficult situations or dealing with some painful fact or reality in their life. This book is meant to remind you that no matter what you face, or what you go through, there is never a time when God is not at work in you and at work on your behalf. In fact, beloved, right now while you are hurting, right now while your heart is breaking, right now in the midst of your pain and your questions, God is at work.

## Other Books by
## Bishop Timothy J. Clarke

*Caution! God at Work—Trusting God through tough times*

*Celebrating the Family: Lessons from the Book of Ruth*

*Living in the Blessed Place*

*Making the Most of Your Time*

*The Price of Victory: Strategies for winning a faith fight*

*Reclaim Your Spiritual Health*

*To My Sisters Beloved: A trilogy of encouragement*

www.ingramcontent.com/pod-product-compliance
Lightning Source LLC
Chambersburg PA
CBHW060523030426
42337CB00015B/1977